Quarterback John Elway

FOOTBALL'S ERA OF DEFENSE

Linebacker Ray Lewis

NFL SUPER BOWL STORIES

FOOTBALL'S ERA OF DEFENSE

(1995–2004)

JASON OLSON

CREATIVE SPORTS

Defensive lineman Reggie White

CREATIVE EDUCATION / CREATIVE PAPERBACKS

Published by Creative Education and Creative Paperbacks
P.O. Box 227, Mankato, Minnesota 56002
Creative Education and Creative Paperbacks are imprints of The Creative Company
www.thecreativecompany.us

Design and production by Blue Design (www.bluedes.com)
Art direction by Graham Morgan
Edited by Kremena Spengler

Images by Getty Images/Allen Kee, 15, Andrew D. Bernstein, 19, Andy Hayt, 7, 11, Andy Lyons, 30, Doug Pensinger, 4–5, 32, Elsa, 14, Focus On Sport, cover, 6, 12, 16, G Fiume, 10, George Gojkovich, 1, 3, George Rose, 7, Jon Soohoo, 6, Michael J. Minardi, 9, Michael Montes, 26–27, Otto Greule Jr, 7, Patrick Smith, 29, PETER MUHLY, 22, Peter Read Miller, 25, Rich Kane/Icon Sportswire, 2, Robert Riger, 7, Robin Alam/Icon Sportswire, 6, Ronald Martinez, 10, Tim Umphrey, 20; NFL/Vernon Biever, 6

Library of Congress Cataloging-in-Publication Data
Names: Olson, Jason, 1981– author.
Title: Football's era of defense (1995–2004) / Jason Olson.
Description: Mankato, Minnesota : Creative Education and Creative Paperbacks, [2026] | Series: Creative Sports. NFL Super Bowl stories | Includes index. | Audience: Ages 8–12 years | Audience: Grades 4–6 | Summary: "Reggie White, Michael Strahan, Ray Lewis: Football's Era of Defense (1995–2004) was dominated by these names. Dramatic recaps introduce middle-grade readers to star NFL players from this era and ten exciting Super Bowls"– Provided by publisher.
Identifiers: LCCN 2024057666 (print) | LCCN 2024057667 (ebook) | ISBN 9798889896098 (lib. bdg.) | ISBN 9781682777756 (paperback) | ISBN 9798889896890 (ebook)
Subjects: LCSH: Football–Defense–United States–History–20th century–Juvenile literature. | Football–Defense–United States–History–21st century–Juvenile literature. | Football players–United States–History–Juvenile literature. | Super Bowl—History–Juvenile literature. | National Football League–History–Juvenile literature.
Classification: LCC GV951.18 .O47 2026 (print) | LCC GV951.18 (ebook) | DDC 796.332/6409049–dc23/eng/20241227
LC record available at https://lccn.loc.gov/2024057666
LC ebook record available at https://lccn.loc.gov/2024057667

Printed in India

Cornerback Deion Sanders

CONTENTS

SUPER BOWL LEGENDS

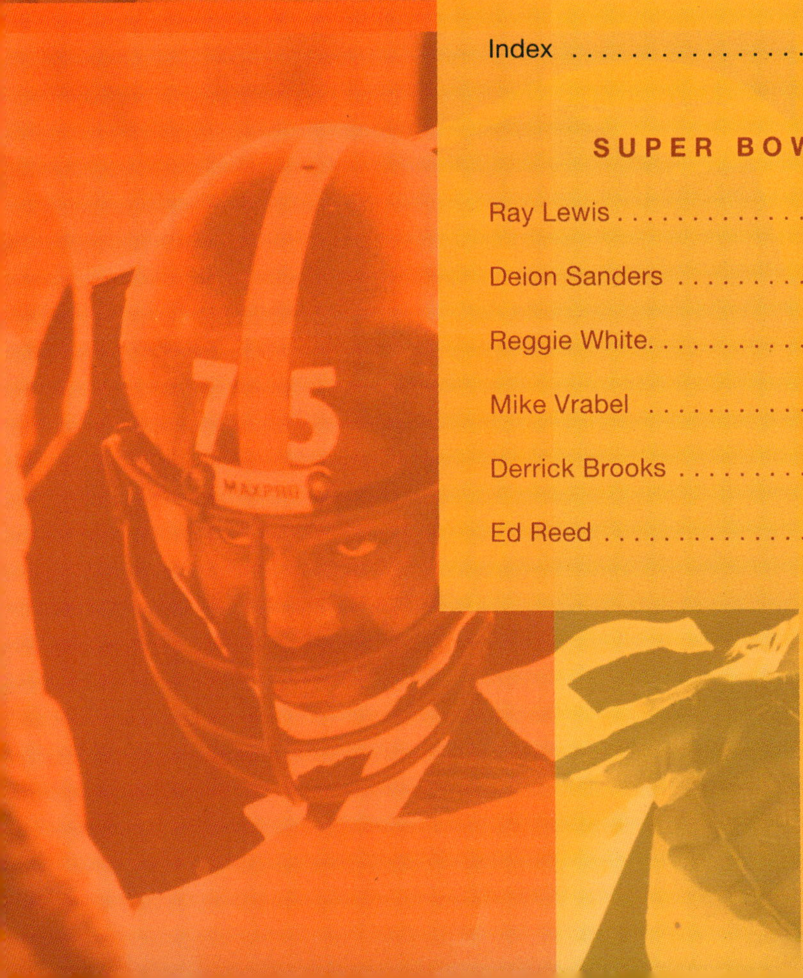

INTRODUCTION

Cincinnati Bengals running back Corey Dillon stormed off the field part-way through a game against the Baltimore Ravens in 2000. The Ravens defense held Dillon to 9 yards on 12 carries, with steady hits by their leader, linebacker Ray Lewis.

The 2000 Ravens defense measures the greatness of all modern defenses. Lewis was the heart of the unit. It also included safeties Rod Woodson and Jamie Sharper, linemen Tony Siragusa and Sam Adams, and linebacker Peter Boulware.

In the 1990s and 2000s, teams like the Ravens fielded powerful, creative defenses. Players like Lewis became the game's most important players. They crushed offensive lines and changed turnovers into points. They helped win the biggest prize of all, the National Football League's (NFL's) championship game, the Super Bowl. Their legendary names and heart-pounding plays tell the story of football's "Era of Defense."

Baltimore Ravens defense, 2000

RAY LEWIS

LINEBACKER
BALTIMORE RAVENS (1996–2012)
6-FOOT-1, 240 POUNDS

Ray Lewis played all his 17 seasons with the Ravens. He anchored their strong defense. He led the team in tackles for 14 of 17 seasons. The 12-time Pro Bowl, 7-time All-Pro, and 2-time Super Bowl champion has 978 single tackles, 365 assists, 41.5 sacks, 20 fumble recoveries, and 31 interceptions. He was a two-time Defensive Player of the Year. The Ravens placed a statue of Lewis outside M&T Bank Stadium in Baltimore, Maryland, in 2014. He joined the Football Hall of Fame in 2018.

Linebacker Ray Lewis

Quarterback Steve Young

NINERS, COWBOYS RULE

Super Bowl XXIX (29) was a matchup between the San Francisco 49ers and the San Diego Chargers. They met at the Joe Robbie Stadium in Miami, Florida.

It was a wild-scoring game. San Francisco quarterback Steve Young passed for a record six touchdowns. He proved to be a good replacement for quarterback Joe Montana. Montana had won four Super Bowls in the 1980s. The last two were with Young as his backup.

Both defenses were strong, with many future Hall of Famers. San Francisco defensive back Deion Sanders was a superstar. Joining him were linebacker Ken Norton Jr. and defensive lineman Dana Stubblefield. San Diego countered with linebacker Junior Seau and safety Rodney Harrison.

The 49ers intercepted three passes, including cornerback Eric Davis's grab just before halftime. Davis also knocked away a pass on fourth down in the third quarter. Sanders sealed the game with an interception with 32 seconds left. As San Diego threatened to score, Sanders snatched the ball in the end zone. He returned the pass to the 14-yard line. It was the defensive play of the game. The 49ers won their fifth, then-record, Super Bowl. The score was 49–26.

The Dallas Cowboys and Pittsburg Steelers met in Super Bowl XXX (30) at Sun Devil Stadium in Tempe, Arizona. Quarterback Troy Aikman, running back Emmitt Smith, and receiver Michael Irvin led the Cowboys. The three were known as "The Triplets." Sanders had moved from San Francisco to Dallas. He lined up alongside defensive end Charles Haley and cornerback Larry Brown. Pittsburgh countered with defensive back Rod Woodson and linebackers Kevin Greene, Greg Lloyd, and Levon Kirkland.

Dallas's Larry Brown became the first cornerback to be named Super Bowl MVP after intercepting two passes in the second half, to Steelers quarterback Neil O'Donnell's right side. Brown returned the first interception 44 yards, reaching the Steelers' 18-yard line. He set up Smith's touchdown from one yard out midway through the third quarter. The Cowboys took a 20–7 lead. Pittsburgh quickly narrowed it to 20–17. Brown picked off O'Donnell a second time, this time stepping out of bounds inside the six-yard line. Smith took it the rest of the way, scoring from four yards out. Dallas won the Super Bowl. The score was 27–17.

Quarterback Troy Aikman

Sanders became the only player to intercept a pass and catch a reception in the same Super Bowl. Haley was first to win five Super Bowl rings, two with San Francisco and two with Dallas.

LAMBEAU LEAPING

The Green Bay Packers faced the New England Patriots in Super Bowl XXXI (31) at the Louisiana Superdome in New Orleans, Louisiana. The Packers had won 11 championships, including 9 before the Super Bowl started. But Super Bowl XXXI (31) was their first Super Bowl appearance since Super Bowl II (2).

The Packers' defense was the best in the NFL. Defensive lineman Reggie White and defensive back LeRoy Butler anchored the unit. White added three sacks in Super Bowl XXXI (31). Butler is remembered as the first to do the "Lambeau Leap." The Lambeau Leap is a touchdown celebration. Players jump over the top of the wall into the arms of fans.

Quarterback Drew Bledsoe led New England. The Patriots defense included linebacker Willie McGinest and defensive backs Ty Law, Willie Clay, and Lawyer Milloy. It was the first glimpse of a long line of great New England teams. Their success would stretch across more than 20 years.

Quarterback Brett Favre

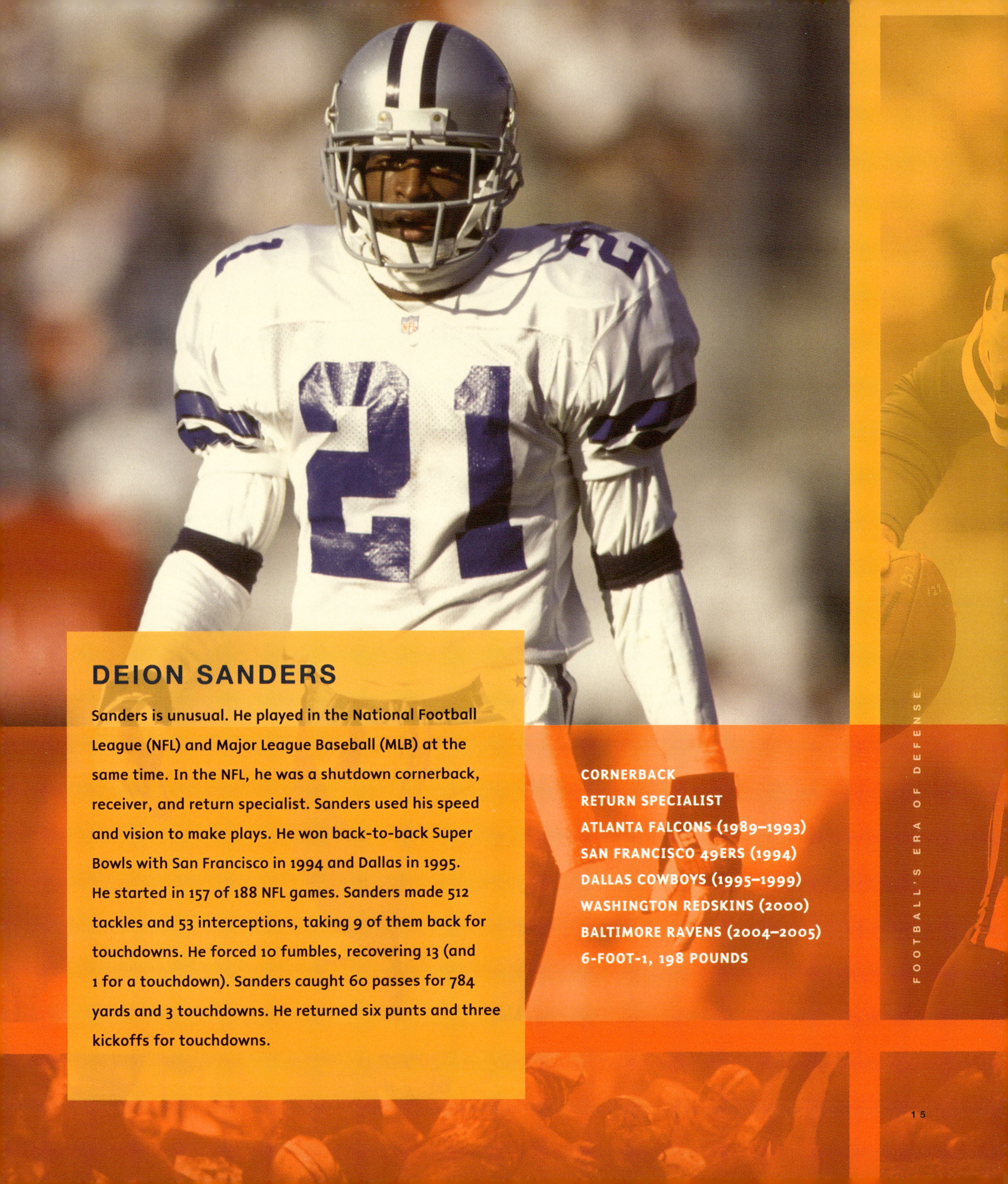

DEION SANDERS

Sanders is unusual. He played in the National Football League (NFL) and Major League Baseball (MLB) at the same time. In the NFL, he was a shutdown cornerback, receiver, and return specialist. Sanders used his speed and vision to make plays. He won back-to-back Super Bowls with San Francisco in 1994 and Dallas in 1995. He started in 157 of 188 NFL games. Sanders made 512 tackles and 53 interceptions, taking 9 of them back for touchdowns. He forced 10 fumbles, recovering 13 (and 1 for a touchdown). Sanders caught 60 passes for 784 yards and 3 touchdowns. He returned six punts and three kickoffs for touchdowns.

CORNERBACK
RETURN SPECIALIST
ATLANTA FALCONS (1989–1993)
SAN FRANCISCO 49ERS (1994)
DALLAS COWBOYS (1995–1999)
WASHINGTON REDSKINS (2000)
BALTIMORE RAVENS (2004–2005)
6-FOOT-1, 198 POUNDS

DEFENSIVE LINEMAN
PHILADELPHIA EAGLES (1985–1992)
GREEN BAY PACKERS (1993–1998)
CAROLINA PANTHERS (2000)
6-FOOT-5, 300 POUNDS

REGGIE WHITE

White is known as the "Minister of Defense." He was a Baptist minister since college at the University of Tennessee. A two-time Defensive Player of the Year, White helped Green Bay win Super Bowl XXXI (31). A 13-time All-Pro and Pro Bowl pick, he had 1,111 total tackles and 198 sacks (second most in the NFL after Bruce Smith). He also forced 33 fumbles and recovered 30 fumbles. White intercepted three passes and had two touchdowns. He holds the record for most seasons with 15 or more sacks, at 5. He had 9 straight seasons with at least 10 sacks. White joined the Football Hall of Fame in 2006.

Super Bowl XXXI (31) is also remembered for Desmond Howard's 99-yard kickoff return for a touchdown. Howard was a wide receiver for the Packers.

The game proved Packers quarterback Brett Favre was one of NFL's all-time greats. Favre made a then-record 81-yard touchdown pass in the second quarter. He threw for two touchdowns in all and ran for one. The Packers won the title with a score of 35–21.

Green Bay returned in Super Bowl XXXII (32). The Packers faced the Denver Broncos at Qualcomm Stadium in San Diego, California.

Green Bay's defense had another great year. White piled up 11 sacks, with Santana Dotson behind him as a linebacker. Butler had 5 interceptions and 70 tackles. Safety Eugene Robinson led the team with 74 tackles, 2.5 sacks, 2 fumbles, and an interception.

Quarterback John Elway and running back Terrell Davis led the Broncos. Elway was in the final years of a strong career, all spent with Denver. Pass catchers Ed McCaffrey, Rod Smith, and Shannon Sharpe added strength to the offense.

Broncos coach Mike Shanahan had also firmed up the defense. The key was bringing lineman Neil Smith over from Kansas City. Linebacker Bill Romanowski and defensive back Steve Atwater were an important part of the unit.

The game was full of action. A sack and fumble led to a key field goal for Green Bay in the second quarter. Atwater's strip-sack of Favre led to Smith recovering a fumble on Green Bay's 33-yard line. Denver kicker Jason Elam converted a 51-yard field goal. It gave the Broncos a 17–7 lead before halftime.

Shanahan kept the defense blitzing, especially in the fourth quarter. It forced Green Bay into offensive mistakes. Late in the quarter, with the game tied at 24–24, Atwater knocked down a pass on a blitz to force a punt. After the Broncos took a one-touchdown lead, Atwater finished the game with a vicious hit. It knocked him, teammate Randy Hilliard, and Packers receiver Robert Brooks out of the game. With less than a minute left, Favre threw a pass, but the Broncos recovered the ball. Denver won its first Super Bowl with a score of 31–24.

Davis ran for 157 yards. He scored a Super Bowl record three rushing touchdowns. He was named Super Bowl MVP.

BRONCOS REPEAT, RAMS STAGE 'GREATEST SHOW'

The Broncos returned to Super Bowl XXXIII (33) looking to win a second straight title. They faced the Atlanta Falcons at Pro Player Stadium in Miami.

Elway, Davis, and receiver Rod Smith anchored the Broncos offense. It had taken Elway 15 seasons to win his first Super Bowl a year earlier. He wanted to win a second in his last season as quarterback.

Denver finished the regular season with a 14–2 record. Atwater and Romanowski made it tough for other teams to score against the Broncos.

The Denver defense sacked Atlanta quarterback Chris Chandler five times in the Super Bowl. Romanowski made a big play early on. He sacked Chandler on third down from the Broncos eight-yard line. The sack forced Atlanta to settle for a field goal and a 3–0 lead.

Denver led 17–6 into the third quarter. Linebacker John Mobley sacked Chandler near midfield. Cornerback Darrius Johnson intercepted a Falcons pass. He returned the ball inside Atlanta's side of the field. Denver kicker Jason Elam missed a 48-yard field goal.

Quarterback John Elway

MIKE VRABEL

Vrabel was a three-time Super Bowl champion with New England. He won All-Pro honors once. He was noted for his many skills, as he caught a touchdown in Super Bowls XXXVIII (38) and XXXIX (39). He had 740 tackles, 57 sacks, 11 interceptions, and 9 forced fumbles in 226 games. An All-American defensive end at Ohio State, Vrabel was drafted by the Pittsburgh Steelers in 1997. He also played for the Patriots and Kansas City Chiefs before retiring in 2010. He started coaching in 2011 with Ohio State, before moving to Houston in 2014. He was head coach at Tennessee in 2018–2023.

LINEBACKER
PITTSBURGH STEELERS (1997–2000)
NEW ENGLAND PATRIOTS (2001–2008)
KANSAS CITY CHIEFS (2009–2010)
6-FOOT-4, 261 POUNDS

Atlanta didn't give up. They worked the ball inside Denver's red zone. But Denver nose tackle Keith Traylor sent the ball into the air. Cornerback Darrien Gordon caught the interception. He returned it 58 yards to set up another Broncos touchdown. Denver scored on the first play of the fourth quarter. The Broncos took a 24–6 lead.

Atlanta scored a late touchdown, recovered a rare onside kick, and threatened to add another touchdown. But Denver safety George Coghill stripped the ball away from Falcons running back Jamal Anderson. Safety Tyrone Braxton pounced on the loose ball. It allowed Denver to run the clock out for a 34–19 win.

The St. Louis Rams faced the Tennessee Titans at the Georgia Dome in Atlanta in Super Bowl XXXIV (34). The Rams offense was called "The Greatest Show on Turf." Quarterback Kurt Warner and receivers Isaac Bruce and Torry Holt led the offense. Marshall Faulk was running back. Tennessee's defense did its best to stop them, with cornerback Samari Rolle.

Cornerback Dre Bly anchored the Rams defense. They made it hard for Titans quarterback Steve McNair and running back Eddie George to find success.

The Titans trailed 23–16 in the final seconds of the game. But they had a chance for a game-winning catch-and-run. Titans receiver Kevin Dyson dived for the end zone. He extended the ball toward the line. But Rams linebacker Jones held onto Dyson's legs. The play is known as "One Yard Short" or "The Tackle." It's one of football's greatest moments. The Rams held on to beat the Titans.

MISSION ACCOMPLISHED

The Baltimore Ravens faced the New York Giants in Super Bowl XXXV (35) at Raymond James Stadium in Tampa, Florida. The Ravens defense was so great that every other defense is compared to it. It allowed just 165 points during the season. The Ravens allowed 10 points or less in 11 games, including 4 shutouts. They were the first to limit the other team to less than 1,000 yards rushing in a 16-game season. They averaged slightly more than 60 yards per game.

Linebacker Ray Lewis and cornerback Rod Woodson were key players, along with linebackers Peter Boulware and Jamie Sharper. Defensive linemen Sam Adams and Tony Siragusa anchored the middle, with Rob Burnett and Michael McCrary at defensive end. Woodson anchored the secondary, with Kim Herring, Duane Starks, and Chris McAlister.

The Ravens held New York to just 152 yards in the Super Bowl. It was the third-lowest in Super Bowl times. The Ravens sacked Giants quarterback Eli Manning four times and forced five turnovers. Baltimore scored first. Their quarterback Trent Dilfer found Brandon Stokley on a quick pass over the middle. A pair of second-quarter interceptions helped Baltimore build a 10–0 halftime lead. Lewis tipped a pass to Sharper for the first interception. McAlister intercepted the ball at the one-yard line. New York was shut out in the first half.

Herring had two more interceptions in the third quarter. Then Starks made the score 17–0 with a 49-yard interception return for a touchdown.

Cornerback Rod Woodson tries to tackle running back Tiki Barber, Super Bowl XXXV (35).

This touchdown was the first of three scored on three plays in the final 36 seconds. Each team returned the kickoff for a touchdown. Giants returner Ron Dixon went 97 yards. Ravens returner Jermaine Lewis answered with an 84-yard score. It was one of football's greatest moments.

Baltimore beat New York with a score of 34–7. Ray Lewis did a little of everything, from sacking the quarterback to tipping a pass and stopping the running back. He was named Super Bowl XXXV (35) MVP.

Super Bowl XXXVI (36) was matchup between the St. Louis Rams and the New England Patriots. They met at the Louisiana Superdome in New Orleans.

It was the first Super Bowl after the September 11, 2001, terrorist attacks. Patriotic themes were part of the pregame and halftime. To show unity, New England chose to be introduced as a whole team, instead of offense and defense. This tradition continues today.

St. Louis came in as a heavy favorite. Its offense could score anytime from anywhere on the field. It had done it throughout the season.

But the Patriots defense proved to a match for them. Defensive ends Richard Seymour and Bobby Hamilton anchored the unit. Linebackers Mike Vrabel, Willie McGinest, and Tedy Bruschi combined for eight sacks and four interceptions.

Patriots defensive back Ty Law set the tone for the game. Law intercepted a pass by Rams quarterback Kurt Warner for a 47-yard touchdown early in the second quarter. The Patriots took a 7–3 lead.

It was a back-and-forth game. The Patriots recovered a 97-yard fumble for a touchdown. But the play was called back after an illegal tackle.

With less than 1 minute, 30 seconds to go, Patriots quarterback Tom Brady completed passes to move the ball up the field. The receivers stepped out of

Running back J. R. Redmond, Super Bowl XXXVI (36)

LINEBACKER
TAMPA BAY BUCCANEERS (1995–2008)
6-FOOT-0, 235 POUNDS

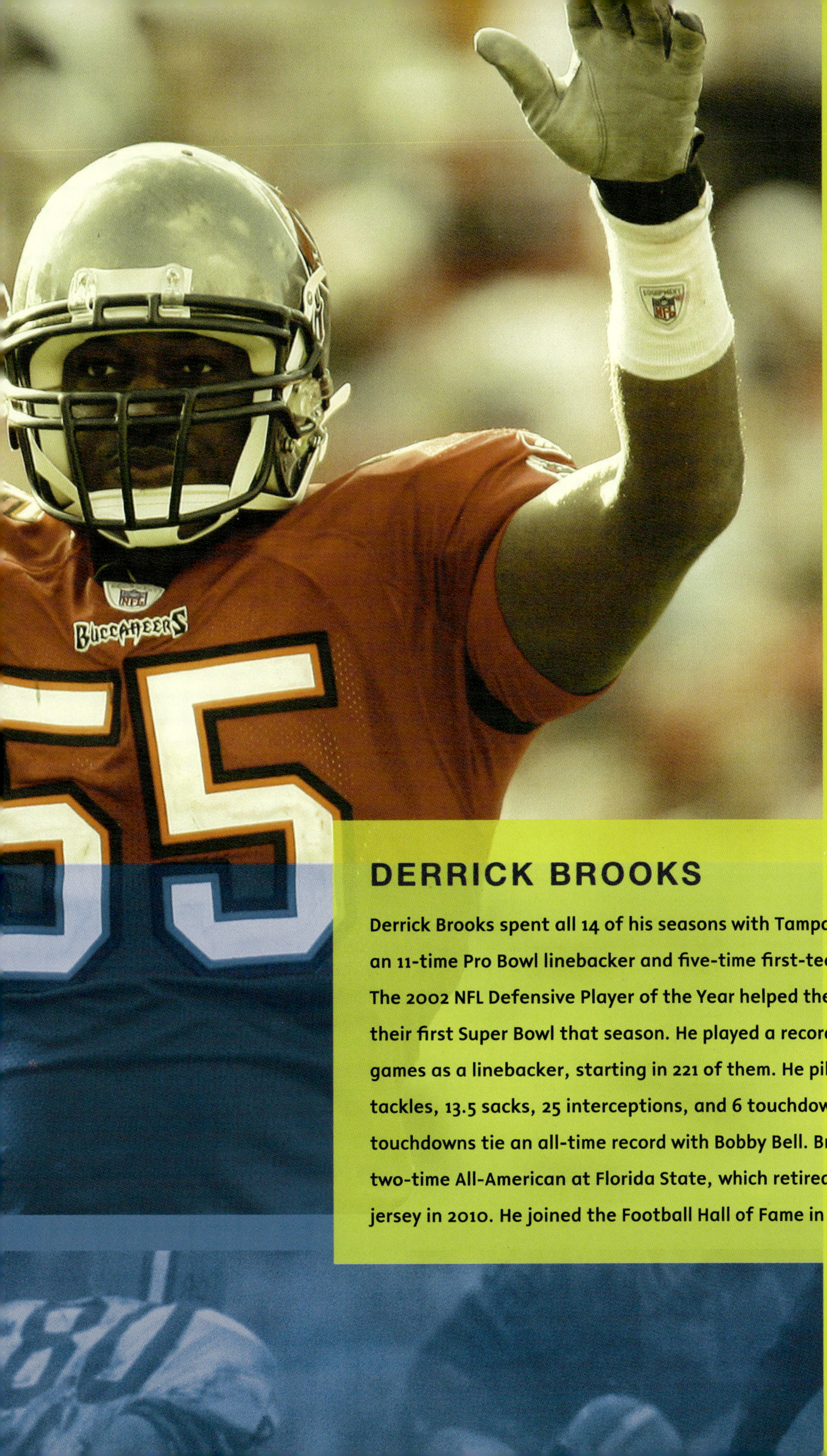

DERRICK BROOKS

Derrick Brooks spent all 14 of his seasons with Tampa Bay. He is an 11-time Pro Bowl linebacker and five-time first-team All-Pro. The 2002 NFL Defensive Player of the Year helped the Bucs win their first Super Bowl that season. He played a record 224 straight games as a linebacker, starting in 221 of them. He piled up 1,698 tackles, 13.5 sacks, 25 interceptions, and 6 touchdowns. The touchdowns tie an all-time record with Bobby Bell. Brooks was a two-time All-American at Florida State, which retired his No. 10 jersey in 2010. He joined the Football Hall of Fame in 2014.

bounds to stop the clock. Eventually, kicker Adam Vinatieri made a 48-yard field goal as time expired. Vinatieri's last-second goal gave New England a 20–17 win.

PIRATES, PANTHERS, PATRIOTS

The Tampa Bay Buccaneers faced the Oakland Raiders in Super Bowl XXXVII (37). The teams met at Qualcomm Stadium in San Diego. Tampa Bay coach Jon Gruden had also coached Oakland. The game was called the "Gruden Bowl." It's also known as the "Pirate Bowl." Both teams' mascots are pirates.

Lineman Warren Sapp, linebacker Derrick Brooks, and cornerback Ronde Barber led the Bucs defense. They stopped the Oakland offense. Brooks returned an interception 44 yards for a touchdown with 1 minute, 18 seconds left. The score was 41–21. Bucs safety Dwight Smith intercepted another pass, returning it 50 yards for a touchdown with 2 seconds left. It sealed the Bucs' win with a score of 48–21.

Bucs safety Dexter Jackson had two interceptions. He became only the second safety and third defensive back to be named Super Bowl MVP.

The New England Patriots faced the Carolina Panthers in Super Bowl XXXVIII (38) at Reliant Stadium in Houston, Texas. Many fans consider this Super Bowl the greatest of all time.

Patriots quarterback Tom Brady was named Super Bowl MVP, but New England's defense again played a key role. It made great plays under pressure. The unit included safety Rodney Harrison, nose tackle Ted Washington, defensive end Richard Seymour, and linebackers Willie McGinest, Mike Vrabel, and Tedy Bruschi.

ED REED

Ed Reed ranks seventh in career interceptions with 64, including 7 returned for a touchdown. His 1,590 yards on those interceptions are an NFL record. He had 699 total tackles, 6 sacks, 154 passes defensed, 12 forced fumbles, and 10 fumble recoveries. A nine-time Pro Bowler, Reed was Defensive Player of the Year in 2004. He was on the All-Decade Team (2000s), a first-team All-Pro four times, and second-team All-Pro three times. He joined the Football Hall of Fame in 2019.

SAFETY
BALTIMORE RAVENS (2002–2012)
HOUSTON TEXANS (2013)
NEW YORK JETS (2013)
5-FOOT-11, 205 POUNDS

The game had ups and downs. The first and third quarters were scoreless. The final three minutes of the second quarter saw 24 points scored. The fourth quarter ended with 37 combined points.

Carolina quarterback Jake Delhomme completed just one of his first nine passes. He was sacked three times and fumbled after the third sack by Vrabel. Twenty plays into the game, Carolina's offense went backwards, losing nine yards.

Big offensive plays helped New England ride a 14–10 lead into halftime. With seven minutes to go, Carolina cornerback Reggie Howard intercepted Brady's pass in the end zone, returning it to the 15-yard line. On the next play, Delhomme found Muhsin Muhammad on the longest offensive play from scrimmage in Super Bowl history, an 85-yard touchdown pass-and-catch. It gave Carolina its first lead of the day, 22–21.

Vrabel caught a touchdown pass on the next drive from one yard out. The Patriots retook a 29–22 lead with 2 minutes, 51 seconds left. Vrabel scored a touchdown on offense. Only one other defensive player in Super Bowl history had also done it (Chicago Bears' William Perry).

Carolina tied the game at 29–29 with 1 minute, 8 seconds left. The Panthers kickoff sailed out of bounds, giving New England the ball at their own 40-yard line. Five plays later, the Patriots turned to kicker Adam Vinatieri for the winning kick. He nailed it with a 41-yard field goal with 4 seconds left. The Patriots won 32–29. The slow-motion reaction to the win is one of football's best-known images.

Defenses were key in winning Super Bowls during this era. They kept offenses from scoring. Their strength led to several rule changes in football. These new rules were meant to help move the ball up the field and score the points fans wanted to see.

Linebacker Mike Vrabel scores, Super Bowl XXXVIII (38).

INDEX